Conten

CW00481937

General Knowledge – page ∠

Transfers 2000-2010 – page 5

Cup Games – page 8

Memorable Games – page 10

Red Cards – page 12

Managers – page 14

First Goals – page 16

Transfers 2011-2021 - page 19

General Knowledge Answers – page 23

Transfers 2000-2010 Answers – page 27

Cup Games Answers – page 31

Memorable Games Answers – page 33

Red Cards Answers – page 35

Managers Answers – page 38

First Goals Answers – page 40

Transfers 2011-2021 Answers – page 42

General Knowledge

1) Watford lost their first game of the 21st century 2-0 to which club on the 3rd of January 2000?

2) Which player was the club's top scorer in the 2012/13 Championship season?

3) Against which team did Ashley Young make his first team debut in 2003?

4) Who became the first Uruguayan to play for the club after signing in 2015?

5) Who was the club's main shirt sponsor during the 2006/07 Premier League season?

6) Who made his debut aged 16 years and 10 months old in the League Cup First Round tie with Notts County in August 2005?

7) Which goalkeeper played against Newcastle in May 2007 aged 42 years and 10 months?

8) Which 38 year old scored in the 2-1 win over Walsall in August 2001?

9) What number shirt did Lloyd Doyle wear throughout his time at the club?

10) Who did Troy Deeney replace as club captain ahead of the 2014/15 season?

11) How many league wins did Watford finish with at the end of the 2006/07 Premier League season?

12) Who scored an own goal as Watford lost 2-0 at home to Wolves in September 2021?

13) Ben Foster saved a penalty from which Blackburn player during the 3-1 home win in October 2020?

14) Troy Deeney scored a hat-trick away from home against which team in the Championship in December 2014?

15) In what year did the Pozzo family complete their takeover of Watford?

16) Which goalkeeper scored against Watford in the Premier League in 2007?

17) In what year did Nigel Gibbs make his final appearance for Watford?

18) Gavin Mahon scored with a scorching left-footed drive in a 4-2 win against which Premier League team in April 2007?

19) Watford beat which team on aggregated in the 2006 Championship Play-Off Semi Final?

20) Which Leeds United player scored an own goal in the 2006 Play-Off Final victory for Watford?

Transfers 2000-2010

1) From which club did Watford buy Heidar Helguson in January 2000?

2) Which two players were purchased from Spurs in August 2000?

3) Who did Tommy Mooney join on a free transfer from Watford in 2001?

4) Which winger signed from Newcastle on a free in June 2001?

5) Who was sold to Oldham in November 2001?

6) From which club did Sean Dyche arrive in July 2002?

7) Gifton Noel-Williams left to sign for which side in June 2003?

8) Which player arrived from Manchester United in the summer of 2003?

9) Which defender was sold to West Brom in October 2003?

10) Which club did Micah Hyde move to in July 2004?

11) Watford bought which two players from Leeds United in the summer of 2005?

12) From which club did Watford sign Les Ferdinand in 2005?

13) Tommy Smith was brought in from where in August 2006?

14) Which goalkeeper joined Watford from Arsenal in May 2007?

15) Watford bought which striker from West Brom in August 2007?

16) Marlon King was sold to which team in January 2008?

17) Which centre back was sold to Bolton in August 2008?

18) From which club was Danny Graham signed in 2009?

19) Watford sold which defender to Portsmouth in September 2009?

20) Who was signed from Rochdale in January 2010?

Cup Games

1) Which lower league club did Watford beat 2-0 in the FA Cup Third Round in January 2019?

2) Who scored the winner in extra time to beat Wolves 3-2 and send the Hornets into the 2019 FA Cup Final?

3) Which club beat Watford in the 2003 FA Cup Semi Final?

4) Which club knocked Watford out of the League Cup in the Third Round in 2020?

5) Who scored the Watford consolation goal in the 4-1 FA Cup Semi Final defeat to Manchester United in 2007?

6) Who scored the only goal for Manchester United as they beat Watford 1-0 in the FA Cup Third Round in 2021?

7) Watford beat Southampton in the League Cup Fourth Round in 2004 by what score-line to reach the Quarter Final?

8) In the Semi Final of that League Cup run Liverpool won both legs of the Semi Final by what score?

9) Which team did Watford beat 2-1 away from home to qualify for the FA Cup Semi Final in 2016?

10) By what score did Crystal Palace win that Semi Final in 2016?

Memorable Games

1) Who provided the assist for Troy Deeney to score his spectacular winner in the Championship Play-Off Semi Final win over Leicester City in 2013?

2) By what score did Watford smash Chelsea in February 2018?

3) Which player scored twice in the 4-3 win at Ewood Park in Division One in September 2000?

4) Who scored the only goal in the 1-0 win over Luton Town in September 2020?

5) Which team did Watford beat to register their first win of the Premier League season in November 2006?

6) Which player scored a brace in the 3-0 win over Liverpool in February 2020?

7) What was the final score as Watford claimed a memorable victory over Leeds in the Championship at Elland Road in November 2012?

8) Who scored the late winner in the 4-3 win at Bolton in the Championship in February 2015?

9) Which team did Watford beat 3-2 away from home on the opening day of the 2010/11 Championship season?

10) Who opened the scoring in the 6-0 win over Bristol City in 2021?

Red Cards

1) Who was sent off for a tussle with Manchester United's Nicky Butt during the 3-2 defeat in April 2000?

2) Which two Watford players were dismissed during the 2-1 defeat to Cardiff City in October 2012?

3) Troy Deeney was sent off in the first half of a 4-1 home defeat to which team in December 2017?

4) Deeney was also sent off early on against Arsenal in April 2019 for throwing a foreman at which opposition player?

5) Tommy Mooney was sent off for punching an opponent during a 3-2 away win over which team in September 2000?

6) Who was sent off in stoppage time of the home loss to Sheffield United in November 2006?

7) Which Watford player was sent off following a mass brawl at the end of the 1-0 defeat to Bournemouth in February 2021?

8) Miguel Britos was shown a straight red for a horror challenge on which Brighton player in August 2017?

9) Robert Page and Heidar Helguson were both dismissed in the first half of the 1-0 defeat to which team in February 2001?

10) Who scored the opening goal but was later dismissed in the 1-1 draw away to Bournemouth in January 2014?

Managers

1) Who was the manager of Watford at the beginning of the 21st century?

2) Which former Chelsea manager took over the reins in July 2001?

3) What was the result in Aidy Boothroyd's last game in charge of the club in the match against Blackpool in November 2008?

4) Who was placed in caretaker charge after Boothroyd left the club?

5) Which future Premier League manager was the gaffer between November 2008 and June 2009?

6) Giuseppe Sannino replaced who as Watford manager in 2013?

7) Slavisa Jokanovic guided Watford into the Premier League by finishing second in the Championship in which season?

8) Walter Mazzarri was the manager of which team in his previous job before taking over at Watford?

9) Which team did Watford lose 2-0 away from home against in Vladimir Ivic's last game in December 2020?

10) How many Premier League games did Xisco Munoz take charge of before being replaced by Claudio Ranieri in October 2021?

First Goals

Can you name the club that these players scored their first goal for the club against?

1) Danny Webber
a) Sheffield United
b) Stockport County
c) Scunthorpe

2) Marlon King
a) Burnley
b) Leeds United
c) Birmingham City

3) Lloyd Doyley
a) Queens Park Rangers
b) Fulham
c) West Brom

4) Ashley Young
a) Southampton
b) Bristol City
c) Millwall

5) Danny Graham
   a) Blackburn Rovers
   b) Bournemouth
   c) Doncaster Rovers

6) Troy Deeney
   a) Notts County
   b) Birmingham City
   c) West Ham

7) Craig Cathcart
   a) Bournemouth
   b) Fulham
   c) Newcastle United

8) Odion Ighalo
   a) Brentford
   b) Millwall
   c) Fulham

9) Gerard Deulofeu
   a) Arsenal
   b) Chelsea
   c) Manchester United

10) Ismaila Sarr

a) **Bournemouth**
b) **Luton Town**
c) **Coventry City**

Transfers 2011-2021

1) Danny Graham was sold to which club in June 2011?

2) Which player signed from Aston Villa in August 2011?

3) Who was sold to Bolton in the 2012 January transfer window?

4) Which goalkeeper left to sign for Ipswich in July 2012?

5) How many players signed permanently from Udinese in the summer of 2013?

6) Which striker signed for Peterborough in July 2013?

7) Who was signed from Juventus in February 2015?

8) From which European club did Watford buy Jose Holebas in 2015?

9) Which forward was purchased from Liverpool in July 2016?

10) Who did Watford sell to Porto in the summer of 2016?

11) Which full-back was bought from Newcastle in 2016?

12) Which two players left to join Sheffield Wednesday in July 2016?

13) Striker Andre Gray was a 2017 signing from which side?

14) Who arrived from Bologna in July 2018?

15) Which player swapped Watford for Nottingham Forest in July 2018?

16) From which European club did Watford buy Ismaila Sarr in 2019?

17) Who was sold to Villarreal in September 2020?

18) Which player was purchased from Norwegian club Bodo Glimt in January 2021?

19) Who was sold to Crystal Palace in August 2021?

20) Young forward Kwadwo Baah was signed from which English team in July 2021?

Answers

General Knowledge Answers

1) Watford lost their first game of the 21st century 2-0 to which club on the 3rd of January 2000?
Derby County

2) Which player was the club's top scorer in the 2012/13 Championship season?
Matej Vydra

3) Against which team did Ashley Young make his first team debut in 2003?
Millwall

4) Who became the first Uruguayan to play for the club after signing in 2015?
Miguel Britos

5) Who was the club's main shirt sponsor during the 2006/07 Premier League season?
Loans.co.uk

6) Who made his debut aged 16 years and 10 months old in the League Cup First Round tie with Notts County in August 2005?
Alex Campana

7) Which goalkeeper played against Newcastle in May 2007 aged 42 years and 10 months?
Alec Chamberlain

8) Which 38 year old scored in the 2-1 win over Walsall in August 2001?
Filippo Galli

9) What number shirt did Lloyd Doyle wear throughout his time at the club?
12

10) Who did Troy Deeney replace as club captain ahead of the 2014/15 season?
Manuel Almunia

11) How many league wins did Watford finish with at the end of the 2006/07 Premier League season?
Five

12) Who scored an own goal as Watford lost 2-0 at home to Wolves in September 2021?
Francisco Sierralta

13) Ben Foster saved a penalty from which Blackburn player during the 3-1 home win in October 2020?
Adam Armstrong

14) Troy Deeney scored a hat-trick away from home against which team in the Championship in December 2014?
Fulham

15) In what year did the Pozzo family complete their takeover of Watford?
2012

16) Which goalkeeper scored against Watford in the Premier League in 2007?
Paul Robinson

17) In what year did Nigel Gibbs make his final appearance for Watford?
2002

18) Gavin Mahon scored with a scorching left-footed drive in a 4-2 win against which Premier League team in April 2007?
Portsmouth

19) Watford beat which team on aggregated in the 2006 Championship Play-Off Semi Final?
Crystal Palace

20) Which Leeds United player scored an own goal in the 2006 Play-Off Final victory for Watford?
Neil Sullivan

Transfers 2000-2010 Answers

1) From which club did Watford buy Heidar Helguson in January 2000?
Lillestrom

2) Which two players were purchased from Spurs in August 2000?
Allan Nielsen and Espen Baardsen

3) Who did Tommy Mooney join on a free transfer from Watford in 2001?
Birmingham City

4) Which winger signed from Newcastle on a free in June 2001?
Stephen Glass

5) Who was sold to Oldham in November 2001?
Allan Smart

6) From which club did Sean Dyche arrive in July 2002?
Millwall

7) Gifton Noel-Williams left to sign for which side in June 2003?
Stoke City

8) Which player arrived from Manchester United in the summer of 2003?
Danny Webber

9) Which defender was sold to West Brom in October 2003?
Paul Robinson

10) Which club did Micah Hyde move to in July 2004?
Burnley

11) Watford bought which two players from Leeds United in the summer of 2005?
Clarke Carlisle and Matthew Spring

12) From which club did Watford sign Les Ferdinand in 2005?
Reading

13) Tommy Smith was brought in from where in August 2006?
Derby County

14) Which goalkeeper joined Watford from Arsenal in May 2007?
Mart Poom

15) Watford bought which striker from West Brom in August 2007?
Nathan Ellington

16) Marlon King was sold to which team in January 2008?
Wigan

17) Which centre back was sold to Bolton in August 2008?
Danny Shittu

18) From which club was Danny Graham signed in 2009?
Carlisle

19) Watford sold which defender to Portsmouth in September 2009?
Mike Williamson

20) Who was signed from Rochdale in January 2010?
Will Buckley

Cup Games Answers

1) Which lower league club did Watford beat 2-0 in the FA Cup Third Round in January 2019?
Woking

2) Who scored the winner in extra time to beat Wolves 3-2 and send the Hornets into the 2019 FA Cup Final?
Gerard Deulofeu

3) Which club beat Watford in the 2003 FA Cup Semi Final?
Southampton

4) Which club knocked Watford out of the League Cup in the Third Round in 2020?
Newport County

5) Who scored the Watford consolation goal in the 4-1 FA Cup Semi Final defeat to Manchester United in 2007?
Hameur Bouazza

6) Who scored the only goal for Manchester United as they beat Watford 1-0 in the FA Cup Third Round in 2021?
Scott McTominay

7) Watford beat Southampton in the League Cup Fourth Round in 2004 by what score-line to reach the Quarter Final?
Watford 5-2 Southampton

8) In the Semi Final of that League Cup run Liverpool won both legs of the Semi Final by what score?
Liverpool 1-0 Watford (2-0 on aggregate)

9) Which team did Watford beat 2-1 away from home to qualify for the FA Cup Semi Final in 2016?
Arsenal

10) By what score did Crystal Palace win that Semi Final in 2016?
Crystal Palace 2-1 Watford

Memorable Games Answers

1) Who provided the assist for Troy Deeney to score his spectacular winner in the Championship Play-Off Semi Final win over Leicester City in 2013?
Jonathan Hogg

2) By what score did Watford smash Chelsea in February 2018?
Watford 4-1 Chelsea

3) Which player scored twice in the 4-3 win at Ewood Park in Division One in September 2000?
Micah Hyde

4) Who scored the only goal in the 1-0 win over Luton Town in September 2020?
Joao Pedro

5) Which team did Watford beat to register their first win of the Premier League season in November 2006?
Middlesbrough

6) Which player scored a brace in the 3-0 win over Liverpool in February 2020?
Ismaila Sarr

7) What was the final score as Watford claimed a memorable victory over Leeds in the Championship at Elland Road in November 2012?
Leeds 1-6 Watford

8) Who scored the late winner in the 4-3 win at Bolton in the Championship in February 2015?
Troy Deeney

9) Which team did Watford beat 3-2 away from home on the opening day of the 2010/11 Championship season?
Norwich City

10) Who opened the scoring in the 6-0 win over Bristol City in 2021?
Ken Sema

Red Cards Answers

1) Who was sent off for a tussle with Manchester United's Nicky Butt during the 3-2 defeat in April 2000?
Micah Hyde

2) Which two Watford players were dismissed during the 2-1 defeat to Cardiff City in October 2012?
Daniel Pudil and Nathaniel Chalobah

3) Troy Deeney was sent off in the first half of a 4-1 home defeat to which team in December 2017?
Huddersfield Town

4) Deeney was also sent off early on against Arsenal in April 2019 for throwing a foreman at which opposition player?
Lucas Torreira

5) Tommy Mooney was sent off for punching an opponent during a 3-2 away win over which team in September 2000?
Stockport County

6) Who was sent off in stoppage time of the home loss to Sheffield United in November 2006?
Chris Powell

7) Which Watford player was sent off following a mass brawl at the end of the 1-0 defeat to Bournemouth in February 2021?
Joao Pedro

8) Miguel Britos was shown a straight red for a horror challenge on which Brighton player in August 2017?
Anthony Knockaert

9) Robert Page and Heidar Helguson were both dismissed in the first half of the 1-0 defeat to which team in February 2001?
Blackburn Rovers

10) Who scored the opening goal but was later dismissed in the 1-1 draw away to Bournemouth in January 2014?
Gabriele Angella

Managers Answers

1) Who was the manager of Watford at the beginning of the 21st century?
Graham Taylor

2) Which former Chelsea manager took over the reins in July 2001?
Gianluca Vialli

3) What was the result in Aidy Boothroyd's last game in charge of the club in the match against Blackpool in November 2008?
Watford 3-4 Blackpool

4) Who was placed in caretaker charge after Boothroyd left the club?
Malky Mackay

5) Which future Premier League manager was the gaffer between November 2008 and June 2009?
Brendan Rodgers

6) Giuseppe Sannino replaced who as Watford manager in 2013?
Gianfranco Zola

7) Slavisa Jokanovic guided Watford into the Premier League by finishing second in the Championship in which season?
2014/15

8) Walter Mazzarri was the manager of which team in his previous job before taking over at Watford?
Inter Milan

9) Which team did Watford lose 2-0 away from home against in Vladimir Ivic's last game in December 2020?
Huddersfield Town

10) How many Premier League games did Xisco Munoz take charge of before being replaced by Claudio Ranieri in October 2021?
Seven

First Goals Answers

1) Danny Webber
   Stockport County

2) Marlon King
   Burnley

3) Lloyd Doyley
   Queens Park Rangers

4) Ashley Young
   Millwall

5) Danny Graham
   Doncaster Rovers

6) Troy Deeney
   Notts County

7) Craig Cathcart
   Bournemouth

8) Odion Ighalo
   Brentford

9) Gerard Deulofeu
   Chelsea

10) Ismaila Sarr
    Coventry City

Transfers 2011-2021 Answers

1) Danny Graham was sold to which club in June 2011?
Swansea

2) Which player signed from Aston Villa in August 2011?
Jonathan Hogg

3) Who was sold to Bolton in the 2012 January transfer window?
Marvin Sordell

4) Which goalkeeper left to sign for Ipswich in July 2012?
Scott Loach

5) How many players signed permanently from Udinese in the summer of 2013?
Six

6) Which striker signed for Peterborough in July 2013?
Britt Assombalonga

7) Who was signed from Juventus in February 2015?
Marco Motta

8) From which European club did Watford buy Jose Holebas in 2015?
Olympiakos

9) Which forward was purchased from Liverpool in July 2016?
Jerome Sinclair

10) Who did Watford sell to Porto in the summer of 2016?
Miguel Layun

11) Which full-back was bought from Newcastle in 2016?
Darryl Janmaat

12) Which two players left to join Sheffield Wednesday in July 2016?
Daniel Pudil and Almen Abdi

13) Striker Andre Gray was a 2017 signing from which side?
Burnley

14) Who arrived from Bologna in July 2018?
Adam Masina

15) Which player swapped Watford for Nottingham Forest in July 2018?
Costel Pantilimon

16) From which European club did Watford buy Ismaila Sarr in 2019?
Rennes

17) Who was sold to Villarreal in September 2020?
Pervis Estupinan

18) Which player was purchased from Norwegian club Bodo Glimt in January 2021?
Philip Zinckernagel

19) Who was sold to Crystal Palace in August 2021?
Will Hughes

20) Young forward Kwadwo Baah was signed from which English team in July 2021?
Rochdale

If you enjoyed this book please consider leaving a five star review on Amazon

Books by Jack Pearson available on Amazon:

Cricket:

Cricket World Cup 2019 Quiz Book
The Ashes 2019 Cricket Quiz Book
The Ashes 2010-2019 Quiz Book
The Ashes 2005 Quiz Book
The Indian Premier League Quiz Book

Football:

The Quiz Book of Premier League Football Transfers
The Quiz Book of the England Football Team in the 21st Century
The Quiz Book of Arsenal Football Club in the 21st Century
The Quiz Book of Aston Villa Football Club in the 21st Century
The Quiz Book of Chelsea Football Club in the 21st Century
The Quiz Book of Everton Football Club in the 21st Century

The Quiz Book of Leeds United Football Club in the 21st Century

The Quiz Book of Leicester City Football Club in the 21st Century

The Quiz Book of Liverpool Football Club in the 21st Century

The Quiz Book of Manchester City Football Club in the 21st Century

The Quiz Book of Manchester United Football Club in the 21st Century

The Quiz Book of Newcastle United Football Club in the 21st Century

The Quiz Book of Southampton Football Club in the 21st Century

The Quiz Book of Sunderland Association Football Club in the 21st Century

The Quiz Book of Tottenham Hotspur Football Club in the 21st Century

The Quiz Book of West Ham United Football Club in the 21st Century

The Quiz Book of Wrexham Association Football Club in the 21st Century

Printed in Great Britain
by Amazon

35616956R00030